TOO COLD TO SNOW

A Memoir

SUE A. FOUNTAIN

ISBN-10: 1482585545
EAN-13: 9781482585544

Front cover photo from the Jim Crowell Family
"Ice Skating on Troy Field"

Back cover photo from Percy Drost, 1955

TABLE OF CONTENTS

DEDICATION

For my children, Rebecca, Sarah, Simon, and Ben, and also for my grandchildren. I want them to know what it was like to grow up in the small town of Bend.

...and for my friend Dixie who said she was glad that I came back to Bend because "we need more old-timey Bend people here."

INTRODUCTION

Too Cold to Snow is a personal memoir about growing up in a small town during the time period of 1945 – 1965. This was a pivotal time in our recent history, and the pieces I have written reflect the growing up and loss of innocence of not only me, but the town of Bend, Oregon. I was born in August of 1945 just as World War II ended. In fact my mother was still in the hospital with her new baby when she heard the news that the war was over. She hoped that I would live in a world at peace, and for the most part I did.

Bend was just a dusty little mill town in the 1950s, and my sisters and my friends all lived rather sheltered lives away from the big cities across the mountains. This was before Bend was discovered as a mecca for a recreational lifestyle. The population was closer to 10,000 than the 80,000 it now boasts. In retrospect, it seems an idyllic time with beautiful floats on the river for the annual Water Pageants and ice skating rinks set up for us during the winter.

However, by the time I was in high school, attitudes and outlooks were changing. People were becoming more disconnected from community activities. With televisions appearing in every home, we could view what was happening in the outside world. Living in an all-white community, we watched in horror and fascination as Civil Rights leaders led marches in Alabama and Mississippi. And we watched with sorrow as the bodies of JFK and Martin Luther King were laid to rest. Using my life as the context, the vignettes I have written hint at what was happening outside of our town as well as within our safe haven as the1950s bled into the 1960s, and we witnessed many changes.

THE DESCHUTES RIVER

When I was in high school, I would sometimes take my dad to work at the mill so that I could have the car. It meant getting up early to make sure he was there before the machinery started up, but the early rising was worth it to me. We had a 1956 Chevy with a V-8 engine, and my boy friend thought it was a very hot car. My dad was not a talker in the morning so there was no conversation as he drove down Broadway to the mill gates and then on up towards the big planer building. The road was unpaved and bumpy beyond the main entrance, and as he neared the building where he worked, my dad would make a large circle off the rough road and onto the grassy field in order to let himself off right at his door. From that angle, looking back the way we had just come, the mountains were absolutely regal as they rose up beyond the mill pond and the Deschutes River. Acknowledging that we both saw the same view and felt the same way, he would just say, "Best view of the mountains in town is from here."

The Deschutes River emerges from Little Lava Lake as nothing more than a small stream, good for fly fishing. It drops nearly 4800 feet on its 250- mile journey to the Columbia and along the way winds through Bend, Oregon. It graces the town with rapids and riffles then glides into Mirror Pond where princesses used to ride on large, wooden swans during the glory days of Water Pageants. Now Mirror Pond is silted in; in some spots, the ducks and geese can walk across the river. Old-timers remember when the city fathers and the mill supervisors worked together to dredge the silt in order to keep the river deep and swift.

My father was a mill wright, which meant that he sharpened the saw blades and fixed the big planers when they broke down. That is why he needed to be there an hour before the starting whistle blew; his job was to make sure everything was in order. There were three loud whistles throughout the day which were heard in every part of town. Before the 8:00 whistle blew in the morning, men streamed towards the mill; at noon, the whistle blew to signal lunch, and at 5:00 the workers were released for the day. Hearing those whistles was part of the rhythm of our lives back when Bend was nothing more than a mill town.

"Des Chutes" means "of the falls;" however, when French fur traders named the river that runs through Central Oregon, they called it Rivière des Chutes to mark the falls on the Columbia River, not any of the falls near Bend. Still, it is nice to think that the river is "of the falls" closer to home, that it is "of" the waters that rush over Benham Falls and Dillon Falls before slowing down for Mirror Pond and the big bend in the river.

If my father were alive today, he would notice the absence of those mill whistles, but even more he would wonder at the changes to his town. There is no longer a mill pond, and where the logging sheds and planer mill used to be there are rows of shops and mega structures. In high school we chanted, "Gold sun, blue sky, Bend, Bend, Bend High!" That gold sun and blue sky invited a parade of people to move to Bend. They came for recreation, retirement, and to build a small city. When I left home in

1965, the population was 13,000, and we thought that was pretty amazing. Many other people began to notice the stunning view that my father and I shared on early mornings years ago, and now as you enter town the sign says, "Population 85,000."

After forty years away, I have returned to this place of my birth. In spite of the changes, the silt in the river, and the million dollar condominiums, this town is still home to me. I am at peace when I float the river, fish the lakes, and hike the trails. The mountains remain, the sun still shines, and the Deschutes River still runs through my veins.

WATER WATER EVERYWHERE

Just 11 miles west of Bend, Tumalo Falls plunges 97 feet to deposit its water into Tumalo Creek and the watershed that quenches the thirst of Bend residents.

When I brush my teeth, I just let the water run: brush, spit, rinse; brush, spit, rinse. I have tried to change that habit to be more conservative with water, but it seems like such a nuisance to turn the water on and off. No doubt I developed this habit because as I was growing up, it seemed like Tumalo Falls poured right out of our faucets.

Bend's water source comes from Bridge Creek, which is diverted from Tumalo Creek just below the falls. This watershed has provided drinking water to the city since 1926.

Allowing the water to run from the faucet was also a family habit. I can remember my dad standing in the kitchen waiting for the water to run cold. He wanted to have an icy drink of water, not something lukewarm. Probably a half gallon of water just went down the drain while he waited. I am sure he did not think of it as wasting water; he knew how much was coming out of the intake each day. As a young man he worked for the city water department, and we have old, faded photographs of him skiing up to the water intake near Tumalo Falls to check on the water levels during the winter months.

The watershed area of Bridge Creek is still restricted to trails where no motorized vehicles are allowed, no fires, no dogs. These regulations are in place to protect the water we drink, the water that drains out of pristine, old growth -forest.

In truth, even in the days when we let the water run in the bathroom sink and kitchen sinks, we still knew that there were rules about watering the lawn. My parents both worked, so in the summer my sisters and I were in charge of moving the sprinklers from the front yard to the back, but only on every other day. It was the law that if you had an even-numbered address, you could only water on even numbered-days. As a kid, I lived in fear that the police cars would speed up to our house, sirens screaming and arrest me if I did not follow those rules.

One summer day in July 2007, the water usage peaked at 27 million gallons. The Bridge Creek drainage system provides only 13 million gallons a day.

Although located in the high desert of Central Oregon, the town of Bend prides itself on having beautiful green parks and lawns all through the dry summer months. Drive a few blocks out of town, and you see sage brush and juniper trees. But in town you find the sprinklers working hard to maintain a virtual oasis. The belief that we can afford the excess of this water consumption is no doubt tied to the abundance of water melting from the snow pack in the Cascade Mountains. Historically, this has been true, but in recent years, we have experienced less snowfall. So, even here, in the land of lakes and streams, we are learning to conserve water, our most precious resource.

"TOO COLD TO SNOW"

It really did snow a lot more in Bend when I was growing up in the 1950s than it does now. I have checked with the weather bureau, and it is not just my inflated memory of childhood that claims we had huge snowfalls that lasted for days. In January of 1950 we had 56.5 inches of snow in that one month, and for many years the annual snowfall was between 70 and 90 inches. Since the year 2000, the average snowfall for Bend has been about 36 inches per year.

They used to play a song on KBND, Bend's only radio station at the time, with the words: "So long, it's been good to know you, I've gotta be drifting along." I thought it said, "So long it's been good to know you, I've got a big drift in my lawn." That was the logical conclusion for a little girl who expected big snowdrifts in the front lawn every winter. The thigh- deep snowdrifts I had to wade through may have only been a couple of feet, but the weather bureau supports me - we did have those deep snowdrifts, and often.

I was in the first grade when we moved into town to a house on Broadway, and that is where so many of my snow memories reside. We had a big backyard, and it was always fun after a snowfall to make a perfect circle for the game of Fox and Geese. My sisters and I would not want to mess up the pristine layer of snow with tracks that would ruin our outline. So, one person was allowed to take a few light steps to the starting point and then begin the circle, going clear around and then cutting the circle into a pie shape. After that first outline, we would all work to tamp down the center base and the trail. I don't even remember too much about the game, but designing it was always the fun part for me. I think we just ran around in circles like geese and tried to get on base where we would be "safe" from the fox.

When we tired of chasing each other around the circle, we would start making snowmen or snow angels. I wish I had photos of some of the perfect snow angels we made. In those days, though, parents did not photograph every move that their children made. With so much snow, we made some great snow angels and gigantic snowmen. We would usually have to quit for awhile, go in the house, and dry out our mittens over the register that blew hot air up from the furnace in the basement. Once we were warmed up and dried, we could head back outside to finish our handiwork. Sometimes my mom even made us snow ice cream with sugar and cream added to the fresh, fluffy snow. We couldn't do it with the first snow of the season because my mom said it was too dirty; the snow brought down soot and dirt with it from the atmosphere. I don't know if she made that up or not, but we dared not eat the first snow.

My dad had a saying of his own on the subject of snow. There would be cold, wintry days when we were hoping for snow, and he would tell us that it was "too cold to snow." That never made sense to me as a kid, and I don't know if it was based on any scientific principle, but sometimes we had to wait for it to warm up enough to snow. On those days we played inside, down in our warm basement. It wasn't any fun to play outside in the cold unless there was snow on the ground.

TROY FIELD – 1950

Troy Field, sandwiched between Bond Street and the old Troy Laundry for which it was named and just south of St. Francis Catholic School (now McMenamins' Old St. Francis Brewpub) once was more than the dog park it is today. It was a prime location for Bend High School – then just across the street. We played softball in the spring and field hockey in the fall; beginning most activities by running laps around the field as a warm-up. In the winter, though, it was turned into an ice-skating rink for everyone to enjoy. Mostly, kids came to skate, but sometimes there were adults skating hand in hand, their arms crossed looking as though they were in a Currier and Ives print.

"Mr. Sandman, bring me a dream. Make her complexion like peaches and cream...."

I can still hear the Mills Brothers singing that song over the speakers as I ice-skated on Troy Field during winter days and winter evenings. The fire department flooded the field when the weather got cold enough to freeze the water into smooth ice. When the weatherman predicted a long cold spell, they began building up layers of ice on the grassy field. It took several nights to put down a good base before we could skate on it. If it snowed, the city would furnish a tractor with a sweeper to clean off the ice.

They don't do this today. The winters are not as cold as they used to be. But back then...

Troy Field was an especially good skating rink for my sisters and me. It was close to home and it did not cost anything. We just got our skates, walked a few blocks down Broadway, crossed the Thompson School playground and headed for the high school building on Wall Street. Sometimes as we crossed the lawn in front of the school, the lights would still be on inside the building. One time my sister Lorna and her friend, Marytine decided we should dare a prank in the building and hope the janitor wouldn't catch us. We put our skates on before we got to the school, then walked the empty halls. Dumb idea. It isn't easy to walk in ice skate on a linoleum floor!

"Shine little glow worm, glimmer, glimmer..."

Overhead lights illuminated Troy Field at night, and someone usually built a fire on the side opposite Bond Street. We skated right up to the fire to warm our hands and faces before skating back into the crowd of people who were gliding in time to the music.

It wasn't always so perfect. Sometimes a group of older kids wanted to play "crack the whip," and the person holding on at the end of the line would go flying after the whip cracked. When I was older, I liked being part of that game, but as a little child, I was terrified that someone would come crashing into me. Once, when someone did, I was so upset that I was very rude and snotty about it. Even though he was three years older, I had known Jackie Wanicek all my life because our parents were friends. One day when I was concentrating on skating backwards, thinking that I must be looking like a real pro, Jackie came flying out of nowhere and knocked me down. He was nice about it as he helped me up. "I'm sorry, really sorry," he said. But I had been knocked out of my skating rhythm. "Well, you're not forgiven!" I shot back. He looked quite taken aback as he skated off towards his friends. I still feel bad about being so mean to him.

"Standing on the corner, watching all the girls go by..."

I remember the year that three of the four girls in our family got new ice skates for Christmas. Linda, my oldest sister, already had some new skates that she bought for herself; she always had jobs and money. Lorna, Shari and I all got ours for Christmas one year, but it was no surprise. Lorna, who didn't mind sneaking and peeking around, found the skates stashed beneath the wringer washing machine on the utility porch. She brought them out, and we all tried them on to figure out which skates were for which girl.

The new figure skates were white and beautiful with red and black plaid lining, so much better than the old pair of black hockey skates we had been sharing. After trying them on, we put them back very carefully in the right boxes and acted surprised when we opened them again on Christmas morning. We didn't really have to act. We were so thrilled to have the new skates that we headed for Troy Field that very afternoon while mom prepared Christmas dinner.

As a family of girls, we had our fights, but not physical fights. When our parents were not around, we might throw a screaming fit, and then give the silent treatment to whichever sister we were mad at – nothing really rough. The first time I ever witnessed an actual fist fight was at

Troy Field when two boys started pushing and swinging at each other. I have no idea what the fight was about, but as I skated up to the fire one afternoon, I saw a crowd gathered around the boys and then an adult waded in and pulled them apart. There was blood on the snow, and I heard people talking about the boy who was bleeding. He had some disease, an ulcer, something he could die from. I was traumatized by the blood and the rumors. All I could do was take off my skates and trudge home. The pleasure of skating had been ruined for that day.

HOUSE CALLS

Dr. Harry Mackey was our family doctor for as long as I can remember, although he was not the doctor who delivered me. When I was born, at the end of World War II, Dr. Mackey was still in the service, and Dr. Thom was my mother's attending physician. She referred to him as "Old Dr. Thom;" I guess that is why he was available. All the young doctors had gone to help the war effort.

But, Dr. Mackey was my doctor from the time I was very small until I visited him for a talk about birth control pills just before I got married at the age of eighteen. My family described him as a man of few words; he would come in the examining room, ask a few questions, check us out, and write a prescription. The birth control conversation was no exception. He prescribed the pills, but if I had any questions I had to figure those out on my own. What he was notable for, and one reason why we treasured him as our doctor, was that he made house calls. My mother used to tell the story about how he came to our house out in Carroll Acres shortly after my sister Shari was born. She was born at seven month, quite premature, and when she became very lethargic, mom called Dr. Mackey. He came right out, and after examining her, he scooped her up and put her in the front seat of his car and took her to the hospital. She had pneumonia. My mother didn't drive, and he could not wait for her to call my dad at work and have him come home to take Shari in. By the time mom and dad later arrived at the hospital, they found their tiny infant under a big oxygen tent. Dr. Mackey saved Shari's life.

To have a doctor who would make house calls was a bit unusual, even in those days. I remember when I had strep throat and was so sick I was almost delirious with a high fever. Mom put me in her bed downstairs, and on her way to work she stopped by the doctor's office to ask if Dr. Mackey could come by and check on me. He came over as soon as he had a break from his office patients. Can you imagine the uproar these days if a doctor showed up alone to treat a young girl in bed, and there was no one at home?! Such trust we all had then. And he certainly never betrayed that trust.

My older sister Linda has a similar story about being home sick, also with strep throat, but she didn't get to be downstairs in mom and dad's bed. She had gotten up her nerve to ask a guy to be her date for the Sadie Hawkins Dance that evening, and when she woke up that morning feeling ill, she was determined to go to school anyway. If she admitted to being sick, she would not be able to go the dance that evening. Mother met her at the foot of the stairs to ask how she was feeling. She mustered an, "I'm fine," then she stumbled into mom's arms and had to be guided back to her bed. So, mom just called Dr. Mackey and asked if he could come by when he had time. According to Linda, he came in the house later that morning and started calling her name; mom must have told him she was upstairs because he walked right to the bottom of the stairs and called, "Linda?" With her sore throat, she could hardly answer, but he came upstairs and found her bedroom. After he checked her throat, he told her that she needed a shot of penicillin, but to save her any embarrassment he told her that he would give it to her in her arm instead of her bottom which was the usual spot for penicillin shots. That was the most she ever heard him say!

Visiting Dr. Mackey at his office on Wall Street was serious business. No toys or games were in the waiting room; there was nothing warm and fuzzy about the experience. His office nurse, Marge, was the epitome of a nurse in the 1950s. A large woman, she seemed even larger with the big, white nurse's cap that she wore. It looked like wings on the side of her head. When she came in the examining room you could hear her uniform and stockings making a swishing noise; she was very official. She was the one who took our temperature and gave us shots when we needed them. I remember being rather frightened of her, but I am sure she was a very nice lady. She was just a no-nonsense professional. We would give her all the information about why we were there to see the doctor; usually it was pretty minor stuff like a head cold or constipation. Then Dr. Mackey would come in to examine us. In his office, he always wore a head band with a round mirror on it that he could flip down over his right eye. He would peer through a small hole in the center while shining a light in our ears, nose, or throat. It worked as a reflector to illuminate the area of concern. With the advent of small, powerful lights, doctors no longer use the reflectors that were once an iconic part of their uniform.

I don't remember that we had any medical cards to show when we went to see the doctor. We just went in, had the checkup and left. Mother made a regular twenty dollar per month payment to that office, and I don't think it was ever an issue. Of course, all four of us did have to go to the hospital to have our tonsils out, and that must have been a bit of an expense. In those days, it was very common for kids to have tonsillectomies whether there was an infection or not. We did not stay overnight, just in for the procedure in the morning and out by five. If Dr. Mackey said it needed to be done, there was no questioning his decision. He was our doctor.

MAME AND ROSIE

A few years ago there was an article in the Living section of *The Bend Bulletin* about a young couple who had remodeled an early Bend craftsman house. It was a typical story about finding a gem of a house and completely remodeling it without changing the basic shape of the outside. As I looked at the picture of the little house and checked the address, I realized that the house being described was Mame and Rosie's whorehouse across the street from where I grew up on Broadway. We considered it to be an absolute shack in those days, and now it is a lovely craftsman cottage. I got such a kick out of the article that I made copies and sent them to my sisters so they could enjoy the humor of it with me.

I was six when we moved to our big house on Broadway, and my sister Lorna was nine. Being three years older than I, she knew (or thought she knew) all about the ways of the world. She was the one who told me about sex and having monthly periods; both were topics that I thought she lied to me about. After we lived in the Broadway house for a few years, she announced to me that the ladies who lived across the street were "hores" and that their house was a "hore" house. I had no idea what that meant, but we watched that house with interest and wondered what went on there. Somehow we knew the names of the ladies, Mame and her mother, Rosie, but we rarely saw them until late afternoon when they would leave their house to walk downtown. They were friendly and would wave to us, but we knew there was something wrong about being friendly with them. I suppose we heard my parents or someone say that when they left home they headed for one of the bars down on Bond Street. In those days, Bond Street was off-limits for children and respectable folks. We only walked on Wall Street when we went downtown.

Mame and Rosie were the mythic figures of my youth in the way that Boo Radley was for Scout and Jem in *To Kill a Mockingbird*. We spied on them, made up stories about them, but did not walk on the sidewalk in front of their house. We cut across the street diagonally to go to the grocery store on the corner. Sometimes we saw Mame go to that grocery store and come home with a bag that looked like it held a six-pack of beer. Not that we knew much about beer, as our dad was pretty much a non-drinker. On a hot summer day he might buy a six-pack, drink one and the remainder would be in the refrigerator the rest of the summer. But Mame and Rosie obviously drank more beer than that.

One year, on Halloween, Lorna thought we should trick or treat at their house. No way was I going to go with her, but I watched from across the street. She knocked on the door, and Mame opened it holding a bowl of candy. Lorna stood there and talked for a minute, and then she went in their house. I was beside myself until she came out. When she came back across the street, she had a whole bunch of candy because she was the only kid who went to their house. And why did she go inside? It seems that Mame asked her if she would give her friend a kiss on the cheek. Lorna claimed that she went right over and kissed him and then walked out–with all that candy. "Just don't tell mom that I went in there," was her cautionary remark.

This mother and daughter team was not glamorous by any means. They wore very dowdy, ordinary clothes. Mame may have been attractive when she was younger. She had strawberry blonde hair that was turning gray, and she usually wore it pulled back into a pony-tail. Her mother didn't look that much older than Mame, but I suppose they were twenty years apart. My mother told us that Mame had graduated from Bend High School in the same class as my Aunt Violet, and they actually knew each other. That didn't seem possible either. How could my aunt know these women who went to bars and were hores?

After Lorna told me what their occupation was, she felt it her duty to explain what it involved. Once again, I did not believe her. Why would anyone want to have sex with those women? I was still in the Doris Day world of romances that involved falling in love and kissing someone. That was it. Then you got married and children appeared. Here were these older, unattractive women, finding men who would pay them money to have sex. I did not get it, nor did I really want to know too much more. One time, on a legendary warm day, my dad went across the street to the apartments next to Mame and Rosie and sat on the porch with the man who lived there and had a beer with him. That was pretty strange right there, but then Mame came over and joined them for a beer. I was terrified for my dad and thought we should go drag him home. Surely he did not know how close he was to sin and evil.

Later on in my teenage years, we heard that Rosie had actually gotten married to some older man who owned a house down along the river. For all I know it is the house I now live in. Mame continued to live in the little shack across the street from us and continued her walks to town every evening. I finally came across the word "whore" in a novel I was reading, and for an instant I wondered what a whore was? I laughed to myself when I realized how I had been visualizing the word incorrectly all those years.

Bend was a mill town, and we lived near the mill. Looking back, I can see that those women provided a service for some of the men who may not have had wives. I have heard that there were quite a few houses of ill-repute in Bend, and Mame and Rosie were probably quite respectable within their profession.

HOME PERMANENTS

Today is September first, and it feels like it. Though it is warm and sunny, there is a cooling breeze that blows in and out. Sit in the sun for awhile and it feels hot, but move around and you notice that the air is different, the trees are whispering that it is nearing time to shed their leaves. When I was young, I always felt like summer ended right after my birthday on August 11, and now I see that I was pretty much right. Not only is the excitement and expectation of a birthday gone, but the angle of the sun begins to change and the days begin to shorten.

Aside from the change in the weather, there was also the lead up to the start of school. Not only did we shop for new clothes and school supplies, but my sisters and I all had to line up for our annual home permanent. I think that style finally ended by the time the 1960s rolled around, thank goodness, but before then my mother would get out her set of curlers and start shopping for a good bargain on Toni or Lilt home permanent kits.

To this day, when I enter a beauty salon, I still recognize the sharp, chemical smell of the solution that my mom used on our hair. Once she had us soaked with the solution, she would get out little end papers to wrap around each lock of hair that she wound onto the rods. The rods were very skinny curlers that looked like the bones of a chicken wing, and they had rubber bands to help secure them into our hair. After getting all those curlers tightly rolled up on our heads, she would pour more solution on, and then we had to wait. That was the worst part. We had to sit still with a plastic wrap and a towel around our heads for what seemed like hours. We kept an extra towel handy to mop up any solution that ran down our faces. It was especially important to prevent it from getting in our eyes where it would sting unbearably. This procedure usually took place on a perfectly nice day when we just wanted to be outside enjoying the last days of summer.

When enough time passed, my mom would unwrap one curler to check to see if it was bouncy or somehow magically curly enough for her to pronounce the hair was done. Then the curlers could come out and the neutralizer would be poured through our hair. After that, pin curls. That's right, this was before the days of big curlers, so mother would pin curl our hair to control the new ringlets, and we could go play until our hair dried.

According to the style of the day, having some curl in your hair was a good thing, and if you were like my three sisters who all had very fine, stick-straight hair, permanents were the only way to have any style and body. But for me, it was a disaster because I already had naturally curly hair. For Linda, Lorna, and Shari, the curly perms only lasted a few months, if that, but, I had tight curls all year long. I think my mother was so pleased that the permanents worked on at least one of us that she did not stop to think how ridiculous I looked. When I started school in the seventh grade, a very sensitive time for a girl, Tony Hunkapillar called me Zombie Sue. He had been my boyfriend in the sixth grade, but I think the tight, fuzzy hair-do put him off as we entered junior high.

One time, after a morning permanent, we all went to a Labor Day picnic out at Shevlin Park, and I hated the way I looked. One of mom's friends tried to cheer me up by saying that my new "poodle" hairdo was just like Polly Bergen's who was on the popular game show in the 1950s, *To Tell the Truth.* I checked her hair out the next time that show was on TV, and my hair did not look like Polly Bergen's! She looked cute and perky with short, soft curls all over her head. I just looked like Zombie Sue.

7th grade school photo

WRINGER WASHING MACHINE

The wringer washing machine was the center of Saturday morning activity for my family. I am serious; this is not a joke or an exaggeration. We only did the laundry one day a week, and it was a big project, so Saturday had to be wash day. Nowadays you can just throw in a load of laundry on your way out the door and put it in the dryer when you come back home. Not so with a wringer washer; it was a "hands-on" machine.

In the winter, we would open the door to the utility porch first thing in the morning so the room could warm up. Sometimes we even had frozen pipes to contend with. While the utility porch warmed up we would begin gathering up the laundry. Strip the beds, bring down the sheets and towels, and grab the laundry basket from the upstairs hall as well as from the hamper in mom and dad's room. The "we" I am referring to would be whichever girls were at home. Mom worked six days a week, so the laundry job was ours to do, and we were expected to do it right. We filled the washer with hot, soapy water, and then we would fill the two laundry trays with rinse water. The washer itself was an open container with an agitator in the center which was started up with a click of the switch. The first

27

rinse got most of the soap out of the clothes, and we put bluing in the second rinse. The bluing was supposed to make the sheets extra white even though we also used bleach in the soapy water.

Once the washer and the tubs were all filled and ready, we began the sorting process according to Mom's rules: start with the dishtowels and dish cloths first so they would be germ free, then wash the underwear. With four girls in the family we always had a lot of underwear to wash. Sheets and towels went in next, and by the time we got to the colored clothes, the bleach seemed to be gone from the water. The last things to go in were dad's work clothes and his greasy overalls. Each load had to be put through the wringer into the tray with the first rinse water. As soon as that was done, we added another load to the washer, and then put the rinsed load into the second rinse water before wringing them out into the clothes basket. It had to be well choreographed to be efficient. The idea was to not waste time or let the wash water get too cold. There were some tricks to learn such as how to put clothes through the wringer. Flat items like towels were no problem, but blouses with buttons had to be folded over and wrung out carefully or the buttons could break or pop off.

It was really a two-person job. Once there was a basket of wet clothes ready to be hung up to dry, one person needed to take the clothes outside to the clothesline, or in the winter we would hang everything in the basement. There was usually a certain amount of arguing over whose turn it was to wash and whose turn it was to hang the clothes. I actually liked hanging the clothes outside, but I wanted it to be organized, no slopping things over the line without clothespins on them. I hung the towels and sheets very neatly in a row with everything sharing at least one pin. The underwear never was hung on the front line. No, we hid it on the line between the billowing sheets and the row of towels.

It really did take all morning to get the wash out on the line, empty out the machine and laundry trays, wash everything out, and roll the machine back against the wall for the next Saturday. The clothes dried quickly in the high desert sun, and later in the day, we had to take everything down and fold it. Again, it was good to have someone help when it came to folding the sheets. I grew up with that clean smell of air-dried laundry, and I was surprised later in life to find that clothes dried in a dryer lacked that smell. It was just one of the trade-offs of making laundry an easier job to do.

Wringer Washing Machine cica 1950

FIRST GARDEN

Marigolds don't even smell good.
In fact, we plant them with the vegetables
to scare away the bugs and worms.
Their pungency is that strong.

Yet, they were my first flower so,
I add them to my garden every year.
When I was nine I begged for seeds,
wanting to plant, wanting my own flowers.
My mother gave me marigold seeds,
Ones she didn't care about.

I spent hours digging up a small patch,
Sifting through the dirt, planting the feathery seeds,
watering them everyday. High desert volcanic soil
does not hold the moisture well.
My father, raised in the Willamette Valley,
Said it was worthless for a garden.

But, my seeds sprouted quickly, and with the warm sun
orange and yellow flowers appeared and kept appearing.
My parents smiled and patted me, Susie had a garden.
I had become a gardener.

FROM RADIO TO TELEVISION

Last week Patsy and Danny's house burned down. I heard about it on the morning news, and I felt compelled to drive by and see for myself. I couldn't get very close because the street was blocked off, but I was able to verify that it was their house going up in flames. Patsy and Danny and their parents have not lived there for fifty years, but to me it is still their house. I grew up down the block from them on Broadway, and my sister Shari and I spent a lot of time playing with both Patsy and her brother, Danny. They sold nightcrawlers, and sometimes after dark, we would go to their house and help them pick worms from the freshly watered lawns nearby. During the day, we made forts in the rafters over their garage where there was a maze of little hiding spots for us to explore.

Mainly, though I remember going to Patsy and Danny's house to watch television.

I am guessing it was about 1955 when Patsy and Danny's parents bought the first TV set on our block. That was a huge event, and we would beg to go watch it in the evening. My mother was sure that we were being pests (we probably were) but the excitement over watching a television program - any program - obscured any sense of the polite behavior with which we were raised. Patsy and Danny's parents really didn't seem to mind; maybe they accepted it as the price you pay for getting the first TV set in the neighborhood. In those early days, people turned out the lights to watch TV, as if they were in a movie theater. So we would sit on the floor in the darkened living room in front of the screen and watch whatever was on. The only light was from the TV lamp on the top of the set. I vividly remember watching the *Gillette Cavalcade of Sports!* Boxing was a big deal, and though we knew nothing about it, we never missed those Friday night fights. It was so new to me that I asked one time why we could see the fighter's underwear. The white band at the top of their shorts looked like underwear to me. My question got a big laugh from everyone, especially from Patsy and Danny's father.

Within the next year, my father gave in and bought a television for our home, so then we had our own entertainment center, and we no longer went to Patsy and Danny's house so much. It turned out that my dad also liked the Friday night fights.

Before the age of television, however, we were well entertained with our own games, imaginations, comic books, library books, and listening to radio programs after school. I am sure it is hard for people who have grown up with television from day one to imagine how much we enjoyed the radio. We had a Philco radio that sat in a big cabinet with a built-in phonograph player. After school we would get right down on the floor in front of the radio. *Sergeant Preston of the Yukon* was the first show of the afternoon, and we could absolutely visualize the action as the wind whistled through the snowy Canadian forests. "On, King, on you big huskies," he would call out to the dogsled team. There were also several Westerns: Roy Rogers had a show with Dale Evans, Queen of the Cowgirls, and there was Rin-Tin-Tin, which was about a boy and a dog that lived at a military fort somewhere in the west. My favorite, though, was *Wild Bill Hickock*. He was so heroic, and I knew he was handsome because I saw a picture of Guy Madison who was the actor who played the part of Wild Bill. His sidekick was named, Jingles played by Andy Devine, and they were an unbeatable team. I loved that show, and when we played cowboys, I always got to be Wild Bill. There were other shows that my mother and my older sister listened to like *Nick Carter, Private Detective*, and the spooky sounding one called *The Shadow Knows*.

Of course we did have the visual experience of watching movies at the local theater, but the transition from listening to the radio and having a television screen right in our living room was monumental. It changed our culture and altered the patterns of our home lives. People began scheduling their lives around TV shows, and the introduction of TV trays brought eating and frozen dinners into family living rooms. At our house, the family dinner table remained sacrosanct, but we definitely had to be through eating by 6:00 pm so that my dad could watch *Douglas Edwards with the News*.

DORIS DAY AND HOLLYWOOD

My sister Shari and I went to the Saturday matinee every week that we could. Once we completed all of our Saturday morning chores, we would ask our dad for money so we could go to the "show," as we called it then. It only cost a quarter to buy a ticket, and if we had a little extra, we could buy candy for five cents. We walked down Broadway, across Thompson School playground, and up Wall Street to the Tower Theater for our afternoon entertainment. There was more than just a movie to watch; first there was the newsreel which featured top stories of the time; we thought that was very boring. Luckily it was followed by a serial dramatization with someone like Buster Crabbe playing a heroic role that would lead him to the edge of disaster each week. Right when the snake crawled up his leg or the building caught fire, it would end with a "to be continued" notice to keep us coming back. Next up was a cartoon such as *Tom and Jerry*, *Bugs Bunny*, or my favorite, *Mr. Magoo*. Finally, after teasing us with all of the other short films, the movie would start. Sometimes there were two movies for the price of one.

We watched a lot of Westerns in the early '50s along with jungle movies and stories of pirates on the high seas.

But, as Shari and I grew a little older we fell in love with musicals and romance films. Frank Sinatra and Gene Kelly sang and danced their way through movies like *Anchors Aweigh* and *Singing in the Rain*; we also loved *Seven Brides for Seven Brothers*, and classics like *Oklahoma* and *South Pacific*. We could take a musical number home from the Saturday show and work on it for weeks down in our basement, using our dress-up box for props and costumes. Our best duet was "Sisters" from *White Christmas*. Shari and I still break out with that one every once in awhile.

Doris Day and Debbie Reynolds were two of our favorite actresses. We were swept off our feet as we watched them fall in love with handsome leading men like Rock Hudson and Frank Sinatra. Doris Day was my role model: she could sing; she was pretty; she could be funny and romantic at the same time. After some initial misunderstandings with a man, she would fall in love, kiss him, get married, and live happily ever after. It was so simple. On one of her albums she sang a song called, "A Guy is Guy" which described that exact scenario. I thought my life would be just like hers.

Adding to the movie influence, Hollywood came to Bend in the 1950s. The area around Bend presented a perfect background for Western movies, and local promoters encouraged the film industry to visit Central Oregon. They even built a full-scale stockade west of town, naming it Fort Benham. The *Indian Fighter* with Kirk Douglas was the first film to use the fort as a set. He and other cast members stayed at the historic Pilot Butte Inn, and their partying and drinking caused quite a stir in our little town. After that, the film *Tonka* was shot here with Sal Mineo playing the role of an Indian boy who loved his horse Tonka. Richard Boone and the TV production company for *Have Gun Will Travel* came to Bend several times to film episodes of that series. With each onslaught of Hollywood stars and supporting cast, my friends and I would be on constant guard to spot them – even hanging out at the Pilot Butte Inn in hopes of getting an autograph. My most prized autograph was from Ricky Nelson. He was a very popular singer when I was in junior high, and when his brother David Nelson came here to appear in a movie we heard rumors that Ricky might visit. It was my lucky day when I joined some friends to go look for him. He and David walked out of the Pilot Butte Inn after lunch, and I could hardly breathe as I asked for his autograph.

Aside from the influence of the Saturday matinees and the glamour of having real movie stars in town, my sisters and I loved movie magazines, and we believed every word that was written in them. When Tony Curtis and Janet Leigh broke up we were sad, but when Eddie Fisher left Debbie Reynolds for Elizabeth Taylor, we were outraged. We begged our mom for a subscription to *Photoplay*, and when it arrived once a month we fought over who got to read it first. Sometimes there were posters included in the magazine, and we decorated our bedroom walls with those. We grew up in that world of 1950s Hollywood make-believe, and I am still waiting to have the kind of romance Doris Day promised me.

THE ANGEL TRICK

I remember the Christmas program we had when I was in the fifth grade at Kenwood School. The finale featured the sixth grade choir marching into the darkened auditorium singing "Adeste Fideles," and each choir member carried a lighted star. Actually the celestial light was just two paper plates with a star cut out on both sides and colored cellophane taped over the stars. The plates were then fastened to a flashlight, and in the dark all you could see were the stars being held by each choir member. As they made their way to the front of the room, dressed in white robes, they filed onto a set of risers that were in a triangular shape. The end effect was that of a singing Christmas tree in all its shining splendor. I thought it was quite wonderful and could not wait until I was in the sixth grade choir.

What a disappointment to me when the following year Miss Brosterhous, my music teacher, did not choose me to be in the choir. She said that I sang off key, but she had another part for me to play. I was so sad; no one had told me before that I couldn't carry a tune. I loved to sing, but I had to be satisfied with the other role she chose for me to play. As it turned out, that part was quite special. I was the angel on top of the tree. While the choir members marched in, I came out from the stage door dressed in my angel costume and carrying my own star. Quietly I moved to the top of the risers in the dark, and after all the others had formed the tree, I turned on my light at the top. I was the star of the show, and not only that, but once the choir members were there, I sang the rest of the songs with them. Sorry, Miss Brosterhous, I couldn't hold back.

early, and Tamsin and I would wander around the neighborhood. Sometimes Ted Petersen from next door, or some other boys we knew might come by. It was innocent enough, but if my parents had known, we would have been in trouble. Being together so much eventually led to a big blow-up over something rather minor, and Tamsin packed up all of her things and moved back home. By the start of school, our relationship was strained and remained that way throughout our sophomore year. I really missed her, and when we did connect once in awhile, I was happy, but I think we were both too proud to apologize. We didn't really regain our close friendship until the summer before our senior year in high school when we fixed up our garage bedroom again. That was a wild and crazy summer for us. We both had boyfriends and started drinking beer when we could sneak some. Once again, my parents didn't have a clue about what we were doing.

As our final year in school began, we tried to balance our wildness with our school leadership positions. One of our most obvious performances was for a Girls' League assembly. I was the president and Tamsin was the vice-president. We "pretended" to smoke and drink while we were wearing our Pep Club sweaters and very tight jeans. The point was to show the other girls what not to do. I don't think we fooled anyone when we did that skit. Aside from Girls' League which all the girls in the school belonged to, there was Pep Club which was a selective organization designed to promote school spirit. We faithfully wore our Pep Club sweaters and skirts on game days throughout the football season, but by the time basketball season came around we were through with the pretense. We were ready to move on to life outside of high school.

We read *The Prophet* by Kahlil Gibran out loud to each other and thought that we understood some deep meanings about life. On friendship, Gibran said, "Your friend is your needs answered," and we believed that. When we were together, I could confide in her, laugh with her, and feel that I was a part of her life. Today, Tamsin lives on the other side of the country, but we never forget each other's birthday, we talk on the phone, and we stay connected. When we see each other, we don't even skip a beat; we pick up as if we had just spent the previous night sleeping together out in my garage. She has been my best friend for over fifty years.

"EMOTIONAL EQUIPMENT"

The Bulletin, our local newspaper, features a "Yesterday" column every Sunday which looks back 100, 75, 50, and 25 years ago. I always read the excerpt from 50 years ago because that was when I was in high school. The recent headline from a June 16, 1962 column announced that "Inter-school Girls' Sports Ban is Voted." That's right. In 1962 the State Board of Education approved a ban on inter-school sports competition for girls in grades 6 - 8. As one Board member commented, many girls are not "emotionally equipped" to accept defeat in direct sports competition. I guess that boys of that age were considered more mature, whereas they were afraid that girls would just burst into tears if they lost a game.

I didn't know that there was an actual law against it, but I do know that girls from Kenwood School did not compete against girls from Allen School. In fact, I don't think there were any girls' teams in junior high and high school that competed except within the school. We had GAA (Girls' Athletic Association) but they chose teams within the school for their competition. I know that they didn't play full-court basketball. When we played basketball in P.E. we only played half court: offense on one side and defense on the other. The assumption was that girls couldn't run the entire length of the court!

I didn't question that logic; I was happy to run the dainty half court and pass the ball across the line.

Of course, that hadn't always been the mindset. Only 20 years prior with, so many men away, fighting in WW II, girls and women proved themselves capable of all kinds of things. Girls' softball teams and basketball teams were very popular, and women joined the work force in general. Here in Bend, women worked in the box factory, and in the shipyards many women were hired to work on ship building. We have all heard of Rosie the Riveter and seen the iconic poster of her with her hair wrapped in a bandana and her sleeves rolled up. However, once the men returned at the end of the war, suddenly women were sent back to the kitchens and away from jobs and activities that were deemed too physically and emotionally challenging for them. Returning soldiers wanted their jobs back, and they wanted their wives at home.

It wasn't until 1972 that Title IX, the gender equity legislation, was passed which ensured that girls would have the opportunity to compete in sports and other activities at the same level as boys. Today, girls' athletics are a vibrant part of every school's sports program. Playing full-court basketball is no problem for today's young women. And, forty years later, at the 2012 Olympics, the percentage of American women athletes wearing medals was greater than any other nation and greater than the medals earned by American men. So much for girls not being "emotionally equipped" for competition.

THE SMART SHOP

When my sister Shari and I were well-established in elementary school, and my older sisters were in high school, my mother started working at the Smart Shop. Just by the name, you might guess that it was not a place for the budget-conscious shopper. The clothing lines they carried were high quality and on the expensive side. The store was located on the corner of Wall Street and Minnesota, now the site of a restaurant called 900 Wall. From the big windows that faced Wall Street, my mom and the other store clerks kept a close watch on Bend during the 1950s and 1960s.

There was a core group of women who worked at the Smart Shop over the years. My mom was one of the favorites because she had good intuition about fashion and what would look flattering. Shari and I benefited from that talent because mom could not resist dressing us up. I am sure that half of her paycheck went to pay for our clothes. For two years in a row, when the Smart Shop staged its annual style show at the Elk's Club, I was invited to be a model. It was very exciting to wear gorgeous formal gowns, bathing suits, and whatever else was appropriate for someone my age. Most of the models were stylish, slim ladies from the community who shopped at the Smart Shop. If you modeled an outfit, you could buy it later for a discount. That's how I was able to own a snazzy Jantzen swimsuit.

The Smart Shop was certainly the hub of some juicy gossip, and mother heard a lot of stories. If a woman found out that her husband was having an affair, she might come in to buy new clothes for herself and run up a big bill for him to pay. As one woman told my mother, "If he can buy his girlfriend a pair of alligator shoes, he can just pay for my new coat." Some of the society crowd would come in late in the afternoon after golfing and having drinks. With a few martinis behind them, they would confide all sorts of things to my mom, or to the friends who were shopping with them. Those were the days when a store clerk set a woman up in a dressing room, and then really waited on them with undivided attention. Once undressed, a woman didn't have to worry. The clerks would keep bringing clothing for them to try on, looking for the right size and style.

Women and girls who lived in the surrounding, small towns came into Bend for school shopping, and they headed for the Smart Shop because it was one of the nicest stores in town. Wetle's, which was across the street from the Smart Shop, was a department store with a much larger inventory of clothing and shoes for the whole family. In their shoe department they actually had a Fluoroscope which was a type of x-ray machine they used for fitting shoes. When you put your feet into the machine, there was an x-ray tube underneath that showed a fluorescent image of the bones of the feet and the outline of the shoe. I always wanted to put my feet in there to look at my bones, but my mother was cautious about letting me do that.

There were a few other smaller stores like Mannheimer's, Mode O Day, and Vogue, but their inventory was small. Of course we had a J.C. Penney store which is much like it still is, and people also ordered a lot from the Sears and the Montgomery Wards (Monkey Wards) catalogs. Penney's was up a block from the Smart Shop, and flanked by two "dime stores," Woolworths and Newberrys. There were also several men's clothing stores, and we had at least five drug stores in the central area. There were no malls on the outskirts of town, so downtown was a tight community of retailers. They would all hold special sidewalk sales at the same time or honor whatever holiday was near. One year there was a spring sale where each of the downtown merchants prepared a scene in their window with the name of a song to be figured out. For instance one store presented a display which included a spring, a rock, and a clock; the song was, "Springtime in the Rockies." Whoever could guess the most songs by the end of the evening won a prize. We all raced from window to window trying to figure out the riddles. The trouble was that most of the songs were "oldies," and the adults did a better job of figuring out the clues than we did.

There were also several restaurants in the downtown area, the Pine Tavern being the very best one. But for teenagers there was just one place to go, and that was Mabel's or "Mabes." It was just a hole-in-the-wall next to the Tower Theater with a counter that could only seat 10 people. The size of the place didn't matter because it was the popular spot to hang out for many years. Kids of all ages crammed inside or spilled outside onto the sidewalk. Mabel and her husband Everett were great in their interactions with kids. They even allowed teens to charge their milkshakes and hamburgers, or Cherry Cokes and Green Rivers. Sometimes parents needed to go in and settle up their kids' accounts, but usually people were responsible for paying their own bills. It was the quintessential mom and pop soda shop of the 1950s.

One of the down sides to this friendly retail community was that employees spent long, hard hours at their jobs. My mother worked from 9:30 to 5:30 six days a week. No days off except Sundays and holidays. At that time, there were no unions in Bend to argue for clerks' benefits. Women went to work to help with family finances or to expand their lives beyond being housewives. Before my mother worked outside the home, she sewed many of our clothes and we made do with what we had. Looking back, I see her as a woman transitioning from being a 1950s housewife to an independent woman of the future.

JOB'S DAUGHTERS

Job 42:15 "And in all the land no women were found so fair as Job's daughters."

Belonging to Job's Daughters was a very popular activity when I was a teenage girl, not because we were all pure young ladies who banded together in honor of the biblical daughters of Job, but simply because the popular girls ahead of us in school had all belonged. Most of us did not even know what the biblical reference was all about, though we memorized long parts about Job's suffering, his faith in God, and his final return to God's good graces. I still have a fondness for that particular story from the Bible, and I am sure it is because of the Job's Daughters association. Aside from originating from a biblical source, we were a community service organization just like any other lodge such as the Elks or Eagles. The difference was that we were young girls who were guided by our Bethel Guardians. The word "bethel" refers to a hallowed or sacred spot.

To belong, one had to be sponsored by someone in the Masonic Order, and my Uncle George was a Master Mason. He was very proud that four of his nieces joined the Bend Bethel, and that two of us were elected to be Honored Queens. That was the pinnacle of success. The Masonic Temple in Bend is located on the east side of town, but in the early years when my two older sisters belonged, it was closer to where we lived on Broadway. It was a log building near Drake Park on what is now known as Brooks Street but we used to call it Broadway Alley. It was a very mysterious building and there were always scary rumors of initiation rites such as riding on a goat or a pig. It turns out it was just talk. When I was finally old enough to join and be initiated into Job's Daughters, we were at the new building out on Greenwood. No goat riding, we just had to participate in a long ceremony which was much more religious than I had realized it would be. My best friend, Tamsin, joined at the same time I did, and we dressed up in our first, formal dresses to be ushered into the hallowed room. I am guessing that I was in the eighth grade; I think that was about the age that most girls joined. There was never any question in my family that I would join, as my sisters both belonged and Uncle George expected it. Actually, I couldn't wait.

The meetings were held twice a month in the evening, so we had to be sure to have dinner over with in time for someone to drive us to the Masonic Temple by 6:45 for the 7:00 meeting. For the first few years, we younger girls just sat on the sidelines and watched the high school girls do their parts in the meetings and rituals. In the spring of my ninth grade year, I knew we would be electing a future queen for the Bethel, and I really wanted to win. I was wearing my hair long at that time, and the night of the election I made sure to have it hanging down my back instead of up in a pony tail. It was important to plant the idea that my hair would look so pretty with a crown on top. My calculation worked, and I won on the first vote. The entry position was that of Marshall, then Guide, then junior and senior princess until my senior year in high school; I was the Honored Queen of the Bend Bethel.

Looking back, I can see where that experience taught me how to present myself to an audience, how to be poised and gracious in introducing people, and in general how to be a leader of a group. I learned to conduct meetings in front of a roomful of teenage girls and grown-up advisors. There was a tremendous amount of memory work involved during the rituals; luckily, I have always been good at short-term memorizing. Outside of the meetings, there was a need to communicate with the public to set up the various projects and to organize bake sales, rummage sales, bottle collections, and other fund raisers. I served for the first half of my senior year, and then another girl stepped in as queen for the second half. The next fall, my younger sister Sharon served her term as Queen. Photos of the two of us in our regalia reigned over the living room walls of our home for years. For my mother, those were hallmark photographs.

Job's Daughters is still an active organization, but it no longer carries the cachet of being the exclusive organization that it once was. Like the Water Pageant, it lost its glory as we entered into a new era and into a broader awareness of life outside of our small town. As a senior in high school, we were singing, "Where have all the flowers gone, gone to soldiers everyone, when will we ever learn? We were entering a time of changing values; where rituals and pageants did not seem as important to us as the looming conflict in Vietnam and the fact that boys in our class were eligible to be drafted into a war.

JUDI REEDER: FEBRUARY 1962

During the years that I grew up in Bend, nothing really bad ever happened. We lived a fairly insulated life, protected geographically by the Cascade Mountains to the west, and a big desert to the east. Bend was a mill town, and it did not attract workers from other parts of the country. This was before people had enough time and money for the recreation that would later cause the city to boom. But in 1950, there were no street gangs, maybe a few bar fights down on Bond Street, but no real violence in the community. We patted ourselves on the back that we had no problems with race relations as we read about uprisings in Arkansas and Alabama. No problem here, there were no people of color other than the Native Americans from Madras and Warm Springs. Oh, yes, we could be proud that we had no problems. Later, as an adult I learned that there was a law that stated "Negroes" could not stay overnight in Bend. When Fats Domino came to Bend to play at Juniper Gardens, the owner of the club had to drive him and his band members to a motel in Redmond to spend the night. Imagine Redmond being more progressive than Bend.

For many of us that sense of security ended when Judi Reeder was murdered in Drake Park in 1962. Judi was a senior in high school, a pretty girl with long hair that hung all the way down her back. As a homecoming princess and a class officer, she was well-liked by classmates. I remember seeing her ride her horse in the local parades as a member of the Rimrock Riders. She was one of us. On the night of February 3, 1962, she parked her car along Riverside Boulevard, stashed her purse under the seat, and seemingly, went for a walk in the park. Her body was found the next morning face down in the water, under the footbridge that crosses the Deschutes River - the same footbridge I crossed every day for the two years I walked to Kenwood Grade School. Later reports said she had been hit on the head thirteen times. The killer was never found, but there was speculation for years about several local people. Eventually, I think it was brushed off as having been done by a transient passing through. No one ever believed that.

I have a distinct memory of the day she was found. I was out collecting eye glasses as a community service project for Job's Daughters. I was riding in a car with a friend, and we were going down Harmon Boulevard when we noticed a crowd of people and police cars around a roped off area on the other side of the footbridge. We drove around to that side, and got out to ask what had happened. We learned that some girl had been found dead, but no one knew who it was yet. A very visceral feeling of nausea and fear hit me. I had never been that close to a violent death – probably never thought I would be. But here it was right in my town under my bridge. And later I learned it was a beautiful girl from my own school who had been brutally murdered.

A shift occurred with that murder. There was a communal loss of innocence and an undercurrent of suspicion took its place. Judi Reeder had left her purse under the seat of her car and gone for a walk in the park. Her car was not locked, and her purse was easy to find; that was not unusual in 1962. People did not lock up their cars in those days.

In fact, my dad always left his car key in the ignition where it would be handy. One summer when we went on a week-long vacation, my parents decided they should lock our house. We searched high and low for a house key before we found one.

The summer before Judi was murdered, my friends, Tamsin and Dixie, and I had slept in Drake Park one night just for a lark. We each told our parents we were staying at one of the other girls' houses. After dark, we took our sleeping bags to the park, and we placed them downhill from the street where no one could see us. I don't think we slept very much because it got cold so close to the river, and we were so nervous about getting caught. It was a big, innocent adventure by three teenage girls, but we would never have considered it after Judi Reeder's death.

BEND WATER PAGEANTS

It is hard to explain the magic of the Bend Water Pageants to people who have never seen one. Beginning in 1933, the pageant crowned Fourth of July celebrations every summer in Bend for nearly thirty years except for the war years. A water pageant is really just a parade on a river, and Bend was a perfect spot for one. The Deschutes River winds through town and along Drake Park where the audience gathered at sunset to enjoy the lighted procession. Each year, workers built a new arch with a different design for the floats to pass through. The arch was constructed right in front of the footbridge that crosses the river near the middle of the park. An amazing amount of work went into the construction and the lighting. The lighting was quite sophisticated, changing colors as each float appeared. Local volunteers spent many hours on the project to ensure the annual spectacle for local citizens and for all who came from out of town to enjoy the unique parade.

In 1955 when I was ten, my cousin Jeanne was chosen to be one of the pageant princesses, and in my eyes, she was a true princess. The pageant started with fireworks over the huge arch and then, as the arch lit up, four wooden swans began to float down Mirror Pond. The water pageant queen rode on the largest swan, and the princesses rode on the smaller cygnets. Of course, they did not really glide along without help; there was a floating walkway that ran from the bridge to where the parade of floats ended. In the shadows of the swans and floats, men actually pulled them along, but from where we sat on blankets in the park, it looked like the whole parade floated by effortlessly. Just like a traditional parade, various businesses sponsored the floats. Brooks Scanlon always had a big one, as well as downtown merchants like Cashman's, Penney's, and the First National Bank. Often, there were moveable parts like a saw mill, with real people pretending to saw up the lumber. I remember one float was called "Jonah and the Whale," which featured someone flying out of the whale's mouth into the (cold) river at one point. I guess he must have been swallowed first, but the splash into the river is what sticks in my mind. Some floats had music, tunes from a barber shop quartet or a small band drifted across the water. It was great entertainment in the years before television and other media specials took our attention away.

A temporary fence was erected around all of Drake Park, and you had to have a water pageant button to enter the gate. The buttons cost one dollar, but if you wanted to sit on the bleachers in reserved seating, you had to pay more. It was tradition in my family to spread our blanket on the ground while we waited for it to get dark enough for the show to begin. Some nights in July could be quite chilly, so it was good to bring extra layers of warm clothes. I'm sure those girls on the floats wearing their strapless gowns must have gotten very cold out on the river, but maybe the excitement of it all kept them warm enough.

One year we had a terrible windstorm that blew the arch over, but the volunteers rallied in time to put it back together in time for the show. Everyone pitched in to make the annual festival a success. It was worth it for local businesses because the pageant attracted tens of thousands of visitors to the area.

However, by the early 1960s, attendance began to slow down. The town was growing, and the times were definitely changing. I was in high school by then, and it was no longer such a cool thing to be a water pageant princess. Activities that had entertained us in the past were losing their glamour. By the time I was a senior in high school, football games, cheerleading and the focus on school and community events was beginning to seem unimportant. The country was entering a new level of social and political awareness. Boys were being sent off to Vietnam, our young president was assassinated, and folk music with its political and social messages was replacing the pop music of the 1950s. Between the years 1955 when Jeanne was an adored princess until 1965 when the last water pageant was staged, the times "they were a changin."

The question of whether to try again to stage this marvelous event has come up many times. But there are financial and environmental reasons to now consider. The environmental issue, of course, concerns Mirror Pond and the fact that it has become so filled in with silt that floats could not get through it. City and community groups have been trying to decide how to remedy that problem for several years. There is still no decision about whether to dredge the pond or open up the dam and allow the river to return to its natural state. Nothing is as simple as it used to be. Now we have to meet environmental requirements for any such undertaking, and the cost of that as well as the cost of staging a new pageant would be astronomical. It is unfortunate because those of us who remember the pageants look back with great fondness to those memorable days when we had princesses floating on giant swans in Mirror Pond. It was a unique and beautiful event.

Royalty Swans with the Pilot Butte Inn behind. Photo by Percy Drost, 1955

NEIGHBORHOOD MARKETS

In the 1950's there were four stores in my neighborhood. Closest to our house on Broadway was Nick's Delaware Grocery, and two blocks from there, Nick's brother, Angel had a similar store called The Delaware Annex. We just referred to the stores as Nick's or Angel's. Their last name was Peterson, but they were of Greek heritage, so we could never figure out the Scandinavian name. One story was that their real name was hard to pronounce, so they chose Peterson because it was easier. Mostly, we just went to Nick's to buy penny candy or popsicles. If we were lucky enough to round up a few pop bottles, we could trade them in for a penny a piece. Nick would appear from the back of his store to see what we wanted, and he was always patient with us. My mom told us to pick out the licorice pieces ourselves and show them to Nick. She didn't want him to handle the candy first because, as she said, "You never know if his hands are clean." I had no idea what she was talking about; it didn't bother me if he reached into the candy case and pulled out three pieces of red licorice and two jawbreakers. I was just happy to get the candy.

Sometimes we would venture the other direction on Delaware and come out at Congress Market; it was a real store, with grocery carts, a meat market, a produce section, and more than one cashier. If we were feeling even more adventuresome, we would wind farther down towards the river to the Riverside Market. This little market had gas pumps out front. Inside, a very heavy lady worked behind the counter, and she was not overly friendly to us. The draw though, was that they had banana flavored popsicles – our favorite, and Nick usually only had orange and strawberry ones at his store. So, on hot summer days, we would sometimes risk the unknown territory, and go for the banana popsicles. Today, however, the Riverside is the only market of the four that still sells groceries. Nick's has become the fashionable Jackson's Corner, Angel's has evolved through several stages to become Between the Covers Bookstore, and Congress Market is now the home of the antique store, The Iron Horse.

Continuously in operation as a store, The Riverside Market of today is very different from the old market in many ways. You can still buy a few groceries there, but now you can also sit down at a table and have a glass of wine with dinner, or a glass of beer from the many choices on tap. The basic idea of a neighborhood market is still in place. This is where the authentic locals hang out; you can meet people like Dennis or Frank who have lived in the "hood" all their lives. The work crew from the city likes to meet there for lunch, and there is a retired teacher's group who meet at the market once a week.

Recently it has been discovered by a younger crowd who enjoy the beer selection and the funkiness of it. The sign out front says, "The little store next door," but it's growing up to be more than that.

CHURCH
UPBRINGING

When you look towards the northwest from Brooks Street in downtown Bend, you can see a white steeple poking through the trees. That is the steeple of the First Christian Church on Newport Avenue, and it has been a landmark in Bend for over ninety years. Currently the congregation has adopted a different name, but the building is the same. My grandparents on both sides of my family, Fountain and Drost, belonged to that church. In fact the Drosts were charter members in 1921. My father met my mother there when his sister married my mother's brother. After my sisters and I were born, we all attended Sunday school and church there, and each of us was baptized when we reached the age of about ten. Christmas pageants, choir practice, vacation Bible school, and church camps were all woven into our family life.

The First Christian Church believes in baptism by immersion in water, and drinking grape juice instead of wine for communion. As a child I assumed all churches were the same, but as I grew older and attended church with some of my friends, I found there were big differences. There was a tradition in Jobs' Daughters that one Sunday during each term, all of the girls in the bethel would attend the church of the respective Honored Queen. I remember how I thought it would be so grand to sweep into church dressed in my robe and purple cape, followed by rows of girls all dressed in white. It was a pretty dramatic entrance, but the exit was upsetting to me. Baptisms did not happen very often, but there were two scheduled for the day of my visitation, and some of the girls in Jobs' Daughters thought it was weird and funny when the minister dunked two young girls under the water. As we left the church, they were going on and on about it, and I was embarrassed. One girl also said it was wrong to drink grape juice instead of wine; that the Bible said that Jesus poured wine for communion. So much for learning about each other's church.

Later on in high school, as I gained some independence from my family, I began to question the whole Christian package. I thought that the teachings of Jesus were good and Christianity in its pure form provided an admirable way to live. However, I did not see that the people in my church lived their lives based on the principles of love one another, nor did they turn the other cheek when they were hurt or insulted. Instead I saw narrowness, bigotry, and some absolute mean-spirited behavior. When I was little, I worried about doing wrong and going to hell, but the older I got, the less of a threat that was to me. When I was a junior in high school, my honors English teacher assigned a culminating essay project for the end of the year. We were to write about our political, social, and religious philosophies. Mind you, I was sixteen.

I don't remember much about my political and social beliefs, but after I wrote about my religious beliefs, I asked my mom to read my paper. She was upset and truly caught off guard by what she read. I basically said what I have already indicated, that I thought Jesus was a good man, but I didn't believe in all of those miracles. Not only that, but it seemed to me that the Bible was just a good piece of literature, and I should also learn about other religions. I didn't believe that one church had all the answers. My mother was a lovely person who really did strive to lead a Christian life; the day she read my paper was a hard day for her. She felt like she had failed me.

Still, I did not abandon the church during the years I lived at home. I continued to attend church with my family, and in fact, I was married there in 1963. I turned 18 in August of that year, and one month later I married my high school sweetheart. At that time, it was not so unusual for girls to get married right out of high school. I was not pregnant; there was no shotgun forcing us, we were just in love and wanted to be together as we went off to college. My mother did try to talk me out of it because we were so young, but she gave up easily when I said we would just run away and get married anyway. If she had called my bluff on that, I doubt that we would have eloped. We didn't have a clue about anything that sophisticated. In the end, we planned a small wedding at the First Christian Church in Bend, my family church.

MY APOLOGY TO NANCY CHANDLER

The summer I turned 17, I worked as a mother's helper for the Chandler family. Mrs. Chandler, Nancy, had just delivered a baby boy into the family of five girls, and she needed some help. Robert Chandler was the well-known editor of the Bend Bulletin, and the summer I worked for the family, he was running for the office of State Representative from our district. Mrs. Chandler hired me through a telephone interview. She recognized my name because I was slated to become the Queen of Job's Daughters in September, and she hired me on the spot. My job was to arrive at 8:00 each morning and help with whatever chores needed to be done. I started with clearing the breakfast dishes, loading the dishwasher, and starting the laundry. From there I looked to Mrs. Chandler for direction. She was an amazing woman who remained unruffled with all the activity going on in the household. I was not hired to baby-sit, but to help her with the work she could not get done.

I learned so much from Nancy Chandler, and she was so gracious in the way she taught me everything from how to fold towels to how to wash and dry greens for the salad. I really admired her. They entertained often, and during the day she showed me how to set the table, polish the chafing dishes, and lay out the silver for dinner. It was a whole new world for me because I had never before spent time in the home of a wealthy family. I had not even known what a chafing dish was. They lived just east of Bend on a small ranch where they raised quarter horses. It was a thrill to me just to drive down their long driveway everyday and survey the big house and the horses grazing in the pasture.

The girls, Patsy, Betsy, Cookie, Peggy, and Janet, ranged in ages from about five years old to fourteen. Little Bobby Chandler was just a few months old at the time I worked for them. The older girls were often busy with their friends or off to a camp, but the younger ones followed me around and talked to me while I made up their beds and picked up their laundry. If I arrived when the family was still at breakfast, Mr. and Mrs. Chandler would include me in their conversation asking me what books I had read or what I planned to do after high school. I was very pleased to be accepted and trusted by them.

At noon, Mrs. Chandler would fix amazing lunches, not just peanut butter sandwiches, but something like an open-faced sandwich with meat, cheese, and tomato that she put under the broiler and then added a dab of mustard when it came out of the oven. I loved her creative cooking. After lunch I cleaned up the dishes and my job for the day was over.

One Sunday they hosted a big picnic for all of the employees from The Bend Bulletin, and when I arrived to work on Monday there were a lot of items to clean up and put away. In the picnic area there were about a dozen 12-pack boxes of beer scattered about. Mrs. Chandler asked me to sort through the cases and fill up the half empty ones, dispose of the empty boxes, and stack up the filled boxes of beer in a hall closet. She commented that it would probably still be there next summer for their annual picnic. With that, she took off for town. Now this was the summer before my senior year in high school, and my friends and I had begun to drink beer at parties. In fact, my friend Tamsin and I were planning a camping trip for my birthday in August, and we were hoping to find someone who would buy us some beer. And here it was, right in front of me. I had never stolen anything in my life, but I reasoned that no one would know if I helped myself to some of that beer. Obviously the Chandlers weren't going to drink it. I diligently sorted and stacked the cans of beer, all the time worrying if I dared to take some. When I was all done, and there was a respectable amount stacked in the closet, I took one of those 12 packs out to my car and put it in the trunk. Yes, Miss Queen of Job's Daughters stole a half a case of beer. I felt terribly guilty, but I did it anyway. And that is why I owe Nancy Chandler an apology. Though it is too late to apologize to her now, I feel better for having confessed what I did.

IT'S "LAVA" NOT "LAHVA!"

That is the way those of us who were early Bendites pronounced it when we referred to Lava Butte, the Lava Caves, and most of all to the Lava Bears! "L-A-V-A-B-EA-R-S, Lava Bears are the very best," we would scream out at football and basketball games. Now we hear newscasters, newcomers, and even the students at Bend High saying, "Go, Lahva Bears!" It just doesn't sound right. A few years ago when my cousin Lois was here for her 50th class reunion she sat with her classmates at a Bend High football game. Every time the announcer said something like," the Lahva Bears have gained ten yards," the class of 1952 would yell in unison, "Lava Bears!" It's enough to make the Alumni Association want to withhold funding!

People have often wondered if there is such a thing as a lava bear. We certainly have lots of lava fields around the area, and there are bears in the woods near here. Historically, there was an Indian legend concerning a species of small bears that lived in the lava fields, and when a skeleton of a small bear was found, the name "lava bear" was attached to it. I have even seen an old photo of a small bear walking across the lava rocks.

Whatever the origin of the name, I claim some ownership through my family's history. My mother was a member of the first class to graduate from Bend High School when they moved into their "new building" on Wall Street in 1927, and thirty years later, in 1957, my sister Linda was in the first class to graduate from the next "new" Bend High on 6th Street. I graduated from there in 1963, but between 1927 and then there were many other family members who can claim Bend High alumni status. My father's sister Nellie Fountain graduated a year ahead of my mother, and her sisters, Violet and Eleanor followed in later years. My mother's brother, George Drost was a Lava Bear as well as nephews Ron and Dale Hall. They led the second generation of Bend High graduates followed by cousins Doris, Lois, and Jeanne Drost, and finally a second set of Fountain sisters, Linda, Lorna, Sue, and Sharon attended Bend High School. We all called our mascot the Lava Bear.

When I entered junior high school it was housed in the old Bend High building where there were photos lining the halls of all the classes who had graduated from there. I remember finding my mother's photo and tracking down the graduation year each of my cousins and aunts. It gave me a real sense of family history and continuity. In fact some of us had the same teachers even though our ages covered quite a span of time. Miss Veatch was what we called an "old maid" school teacher. She wore her iron-grey hair pulled back in a bun, and she dressed in very plain dresses. She had no hesitation about smacking boys on the hands with her ruler or even twisting their ears if they didn't behave. But she always had a twinkle in her eye when she did it because some of those misbehaving boys were her favorites. My cousin Ron graduated in 1945 and he remembers her as well as I do. There were some other teachers like Miss Linn and Miss O'Leary who taught in Bend for many years, but Miss Veatch was the classic, the one people always ask about, "Do you remember Miss Veatch?"

Following the theme or our Lava Bear mascot, the football stadium was called Bruin Field. I call it a stadium because it had covered bleachers on both sides of the field. I have a distinct memory of the stadium still being there in 1960 when I was a sophomore in high school because I was one of the homecoming princesses who got to ride around the field in a convertible, waving to the crowd. By the next year, the new athletic field was constructed adjacent to Bend High School, and Bruin Field was razed. The bleachers for the new field were open air, and there were no lights on the field. Our games had to be played in the afternoon before it got dark, and it just wasn't the same as when we cheered for the team on nippy evenings under the lights of Bruin Field. Afternoons in the fall can be quite warm, and wearing our big Pep Club sweaters to the games left us hot and sweaty.

Pep Club was the girls' support group for the male athletes who were in the Letterman's Club. Both groups were rather exclusive; you had to be a proven athlete to wear the Letterman's sweater, and the girls had to be chosen for membership in Pep Club. By the time I was in high school, it was open to most everyone, but originally it had been such an elite group that girls would cry for days if they were not selected for membership. On Fridays we all wore our blue and gold sweaters to school to support the Lava Bears whether it was in football or basketball. There weren't any girls' sports teams at that time. The girls' role was to support the boys' teams. If we had a steady boyfriend, we could order his name and sew it on the back of our sweaters, on top of the golden Lava Bear. Gender roles have definitely changed in athletics and most other aspects of life. Most of us agree that has been a good change, but changing the way "Lava Bears" is pronounced has not been a welcome change for the aging alumni of Bend High School.

WHERE <u>DO</u> THE BEAUTIFUL PEOPLE LIVE?

My friend Gayle likes to say that he is just "east-side trailer trash," and that I am one of the beautiful west-side people. Then we both laugh because we know that this competition between east Bend and west Bend has been around for a long time.

When we were growing up, there were just two upper-elementary schools: Kenwood School on the westside and Allen School on the eastside. There were a few feeder elementary schools, but Kenwood and Allen were the big names. Kenwood is now called Highland Magnet School, and Allen School burned down in 1963 and has been replaced by a Safeway store. To this day, at class reunions or chance meetings, people will say something like, "You went to Allen, didn't you? We didn't know each other until 7th grade, right?" As if the seventh grade was nearly a lifetime.

I was a Kenwood School girl for the 5th and 6th grades, and we were not interested in those kids who went to Allen. Once we were all in junior high, we blended together, but we still knew who came from which school.

My best friend, Tamsin, lived on the east side of Bend and went to Allen School. Halfway through the 6th grade, her family moved into my neighborhood, but there was no way Tamsin wanted to change schools. She walked all the way to Allen through snow and sleet to avoid going to Kenwood.

There was actually a class structure underlying this rivalry. Bend is divided by the Deschutes River. From the west side of the river, forested foothills lead up to the Cascade Mountains, and from the east side, the town leads out to the high desert country. The main downtown street is Wall, and it was probably the dividing line. Living alongside the river on either side has always garnered high status, but beyond that the status has fluctuated from east to west over time. For Tamsin it was a step down to move to my part of town because they had been living on East 8th Street. At that time, the new houses on 8th and 9th were owned by people with money, and the west side was inhabited mostly by mill workers. Living in the West Hills of Awbrey Butte has always been considered high class, but down in the flat lands lived the working class, and we went to Kenwood School. Within the schools there was a mixture of kids from every social class, and as children we did not think about who was rich or poor. We played with everyone. Except we didn't mix with the kids from Allen School. And the Catholic kids who attended St. Francis were simply a mystery to most of us.

Within the eastside/westside designations, there were also some geographical areas that were considered better than others. When I was in high school, I figured that in the scheme of class boundaries, I was on the "wrong side of the tracks." Or, rather, I was on the wrong side of Tumalo Avenue. Tumalo runs uphill from the river to

Broadway; turning left at the stop sign you encounter tall houses and trees that line the street, showing off pink blooms in the spring. However, when I was young, turning right onto Broadway, led you towards the mill. The homes were smaller and showed signs of wear; this was the neighborhood where the millworkers lived. There were some nicer homes mixed in with the vacant lots and run-down houses, but only a few. My house was good and solid, and I loved it as a child, but as I became a class-conscious teenager, I wished I lived in the West Hills or along the graceful boulevard that followed the curve of the river.

I had a huge crush on a boy from the uptown side of Tumalo Avenue; his family lived on State Street which was quite respectable. One night, after a school dance, he drove me home, kissed me goodnight at the door, and then I never saw him again except at school. He told me that he was going skiing the next day, which was an activity my parents could not afford for me to pursue. I put together the fact that I did not ski and the location of my house and I concluded I was not in his class. Who knows? Maybe he just didn't like girls; I don't remember him ever dating anyone. But at sixteen, I was pretty sure it was because of my neighborhood.

Today, the west side of Bend is the "in" place to live. Awbrey Butte is covered with little mansions, and Summit is a good college-prep high school. Even the little mill houses in the flatland and along the river have been remodeled and carry their own cachet. The friendly rivalry between east and west continues, and for now, as Gayle says, the "beautiful people" live on the west side of town.

ELK LAKE

Elk Lake is my lake. But I will share it with others if they appreciate how special it is. When I returned to Bend in 2003, I came to volunteer at the Elk Lake Guard Station, which is now listed as a historical landmark. My job was to meet and greet visitors to the area and tell them about the history of the guard station. It was a perfect job for me and a perfect reentry into Central Oregon.

Coming from the Puget Sound area of Washington, I was overwhelmed by the blue-beyond-blue of the sky over the pine trees at Elk Lake. I stayed at the Entrada Inn, the last motel on Century Drive before you come to the resort at Elk Lake, and each day I drove up to the lake, planning to arrive by the 8:00 AM opening time; it took me 25 minutes. I wonder if people in Bend appreciate how great it is to have lakes and mountains within a half hour from home. When I was growing up in Bend, I am sure I took it for granted. My friend's mom could buzz us up to the lake for a swim and a picnic in the afternoon, and I could be home in time for dinner. In high school, during the summer months, we would sometimes go up to the lake to party! There were a couple of good spots on the back side of the lake where we could drink beer without anyone finding us.

Generally, my dad preferred going to Paulina Lake because he could fish there, and Elk Lake was not such a good fishing lake. When I was nine or ten, I loved going out on Paulina Lake and fishing with my dad, but the lake was too cold for swimming. Other than fishing and hiking around the lake, there was not so much for kids to do there. But the summer I turned 15, my parents rented a rustic cabin at Elk Lake. I am not sure why they made that choice, but it was the summer I really fell in love with that lake. We could swim there, and my sister Shari and I were at the little beach in front of the cabins every waking minute. In fact, I have a lovely memory of running down to the lake one morning when there was still a mist hovering over the water. We ran right in, screaming when the cool water assaulted our senses. But we swam on out to the raft that was a bit offshore, climbed up on it and sat there until the sun warmed us.

Okay, I will admit that it was also the summer of a young romance. There was a very cute boy staying in the cabin next door to us. He was visiting from California, and he offered to take my sister and me out in his red canoe. After the first canoe ride, we became friends, and he hung out with us most of the time. The scene from out on the lake is spectacular. From the shore, you see Mt. Bachelor looming over the lake, but once on the water, you can look back at the South Sister, my favorite mountain, standing guard from the other direction. Summertime on the lake, in a canoe with a handsome boy who was probably 15 or 16, young love was bound to happen. There were a few nights of sitting around the campfire and singing songs before he kissed me, but I was so thrilled. Shari, my darling sister, felt left out after that, and I apologize to her (again). It turned out that as soon as he returned to California and wrote me a letter filled with misspellings, I lost interest in him. However, I have never lost interest in my lake.

For my 60th birthday, I rented one of the new luxury cabins that was big enough for all of my family. The old cabins I remembered had been torn down or had fallen into disrepair. I walked around where the cabins had been and reminisced about that glorious summer vacation when I was 15. Forty-five years later, I was back at the lake with my children and grandchildren, and other than the upgrade in accommodations, it all felt the same. The lake is still a quiet one, with sailboats, canoes, and paddle boats. You can hear a few motors, but since there is a 10 mph speed limit, you don't have to listen to the noise of the big water-ski boats. Walking the trail around the lake, you can see the mountains from different angles as you pass through the pine trees, along beaches, and past a few of the older cabins that are privately owned. The air is so clear, the pines smell so good, and you feel fortunate to be in such a magical place.

There is a little resort at Elk Lake that has not changed much over the years. You can still have a good meal there, sit at the bar and look out on the lake, or just relax on the deck and sip a glass of wine. Though the structure has not changed, the action around the resort has. Now they are open in the winter for people who want to snowmobile in for a weekend. I have not done that, but it is on my "to-do" list. Sometimes, in both the winter and summer, they have bands playing for entertainment. Bicyclists from Bend ride up for the day, and large-scale swimming events are held there each summer. I still think it is the best swimming lake around. Cultus Lake is a favorite of many because the water warms up in the east end, but it is too shallow for good swimming. At Elk Lake you can enter the water from several different beaches, wade out a ways and then dive under. The first few minutes always feel cold, but on a warm summer day, you become acclimated quickly, and you can swim out as far as you want. It is the kind of experience you can only get from lake swimming, no crowds, no chlorine, just an expanse of exhilarating, cool, mountain water.

TUMALO MOUNTAIN – SUMMER OF 1964

The first time I heard about Tumalo Mountain was during Spring Break of 1964. My husband and I had applied for a job with the US Forest Service, hoping to be lookouts during the summer months, and we had been granted an interview. My dream was to be on Cultus Mountain, overlooking the Cultus Lakes and beyond, but the Forest Ranger who interviewed us kept talking about Tumalo Mountain. All I could think of was some little hill out in Tumalo, and that didn't match my romantic vision. When I asked about Cultus Mountain, he seemed puzzled that I was interested in that post instead of Tumalo Mountain which he described as the best lookout site in the area. He finally asked me if I knew where it was, and I had to admit that I didn't. He spread out a map and showed us that it was right across the Cascade Lakes Highway from Mt. Bachelor. There was no road up to it, but he said it was an easy hour-long hike, and that we would have several visitors throughout the summer. After we left his office we drove up towards that area and, I felt a bit sheepish to find that Tumalo Mountain is actually a beautiful snow-covered little peak that is fairly close to Bend. I had seen it all my life and never bothered to ask the name. It turns out it was the perfect spot for us.

When the ranger called back to offer us the job, we jumped at the chance. We had to finish out spring term at school, but we promised to be back as early in June as possible.

In retrospect, I don't think we realized how lucky we were to be offered such a great job. Though we thought we were grown up, we were really just a couple of eighteen year old college kids who happened to be married. My husband, Scott, and I both celebrated our 19th birthdays on Tumalo Mountain that summer. We were given the chance of a lifetime to live "above it all" in our little look-out nestled between Mt. Bachelor and the South Sister. The view from there is spectacular in all directions. Bend to the east, and mountains and lakes all around us in every other direction.

When we retuned to Bend ready to take our new job, we had to wait because there was still too much snow for us to go up on the mountain. Meanwhile, Scott needed to be trained as a forest lookout and a fire fighter. It was really his job, and I was just the back-up person, so while he became trained, I worked as a waitress at Sambo's Pancake House. The restaurant no longer exists in Bend, but it was located south of town near to where the current Fred Meyer shopping center is. There was a great view of the mountains out of the dining room window, and in the midst of serving up pancakes and waffles, I would cast longing looks in that direction. More than once I informed my customers that I would soon be living on a lookout up in those mountains. I don't know if that helped me earn better tips or not, but people seemed to enjoy the commentary.

In preparation for moving up to the mountain, I planned out meals for the whole summer. I made lists of what we would need and how much canned and dried food we might consume, figuring that I would be able to hike down the mountain and come into town for fresh fruit and vegetables. I knew that we wouldn't have a freezer or even a refrigerator to count on, so I chose items like canned chicken and salmon, hot cereal and pancake mix. I thought I had it planned out pretty well, but when the time came for the forest service guys to take us up to the lookout, they laughed at the paltry amount of food I had gathered. I felt a little bit embarrassed, but I knew I had counted out the meals and that we wouldn't starve. There was still a lot of snow, so we rode up the mountain in a trailer hooked up to a sno-cat. Our food stash did look pretty small in one corner of the trailer, but once we got to the top, I was so thrilled with everything I saw that I forgot about the teasing I had taken. The two men who unloaded our belongings and helped us open up the lookout were actually very nice. They were probably just a little bit worried about us. As they left, one man shook his head and said, "This will either make or break your marriage."

It was so much fun to settle into our little nest in the sky. That was the way it felt because we had windows all the way around our 14 foot square home that was perched on the edge of a cliff, 7772 feet in elevation. We only had one flight of steps up to the actual lookout as opposed to some that had several flights of stairs. We were already so high up that there was nothing blocking the view. Along one wall was a small built-in bed that was really designed for one person, but wide enough that two could sleep there cozily. We had a wood stove, with a supply of wood in the bottom part of the lookout. Forest Service personnel kept the wood room filled up for us, but we had to do a lot of chopping and carrying. I cooked over a wood stove all summer and heated up dishwater to do the dishes, and to have warm water for our personal washing up. Our refrigerator was a big hole in the ground under the shade of a tree. We kept it lined with snow all summer, and our food stayed pretty cold. There were two big garbage cans that we filled with snow and let it melt for our water. No one had even heard of buying cases of bottled water, the way people now do. As the summer progressed, we had to venture farther and farther down the east slope to reach the snow, but we always found some.

Although there was snow on the slope, up on top, it was plenty warm during the day, and we could wear shorts and t-shirts, though Scott was supposed to wear his forest service outfit when we had visitors. We were even good about raising and lowering the flag everyday as part of our job. He was basically on duty from seven am until dusk, and if there was a lightning storm, he needed to be on watch round the clock. That was the most dangerous time for forest fires to start. As lightning zapped around us, he would site in where it struck and make a mark on the fire finder which was a big circular map that took up the center of the room. In the following hours and days, he would go back and watch those areas for any sign of smoke. It was very exciting and nerve-wracking when he spotted smoke and had to give the men in the field the exact coordinates so they could find the fire.

More than once, tired and grumbling fire fighters would question his judgment, but he was never wrong about his sightings.

We parked our car at the bottom of the mountain, hidden in the trees so that it was not visible from the road, and when I hiked out for groceries or to do laundry, I would get in the car and drive the 30 minutes it took to get to Bend. One Sunday afternoon when I was preparing to drive back up, my dad mentioned that it looked like a thunder storm was rolling in. "Be careful," he said, as I drove off. Not one to worry about a few thunderheads building up, I figured I could get up on top before it would be a problem. Unfortunately I had loaded up my backpack more than usual, so my pace was slowed down, and the storm caught up with me. Thunder rumbled overhead, and then lightning began to strike. I decided that I had better take my pack off and stash it under a tree and hurry on up the hill. The going wasn't too bad until I hit the cinder cone near the top. It is slow going at best because you take one step and the cinders slide you back a half step. With lightning happening all around me, I felt like I was a sure target on that bare cinder cone. I got scared and started calling for Scott to come help me get the rest of the way up. He, of course, was busy checking for lightning strikes and never dreamt that I was out in the midst of them. I was almost to the top when he heard me calling and he came running in disbelief. He gave me a hand up, and we ran for the lookout tower. Inside we had an insulated stool to stand on, but it was only meant for one person, the fire lookout. There were many stories about people leaning on the metal fire finder during storms and being tossed across the room when lightning struck the tower. I held on to Scott while he searched the area. Then he got a call on the walkie talkie asking him to run out to the point about a quarter of a mile from the tower and scan the area on the north side of the mountain, near Broken Top. It was treacherous for him to run out there and back because that put him at the highest point on the mountain. I stayed put on that insulated stool and prayed until he returned safely. The next day dawned clear and beautiful and I had to hike back down to where I had hidden my backpack. In the calm of that next day, it was hard to believe how terrifying the landscape had looked when the sky was black and the lightning was flashing all around me.

Today people know Tumalo Mountain as an exciting ski run and snowshoe trail, but that has only happened in recent years. It used to be that few people even knew about the trail up the mountain. There was no parking lot at the bottom as there is now. Still, we had quite a few visitors, and we always had them sign the logbook. People marveled at the view and expressed envy for us that we actually got to live there. One time we had a whole scout troop come up, and I had been experimenting with baking in a wood stove oven. I treated them to freshly baked chocolate chip cookies, and they were thrilled. It's not what they expected to find at the top of their hike up the mountain. Family members also made the hike, my sister Shari hiked up, and my sister Lorna made the climb with her husband and two kids who were only four and five years old. A classic story from Scott's side of the family was that his mother decided she could drive their jeep up the mountain since there was a rough trail. On the day of Scott's birthday in July she loaded up cake and ice cream and all of Scott's brothers and barreled right up that trail.

She took a run at the cinder cone on top, but couldn't make it, so they climbed out and left the jeep where it was, tipped nearly on its side, and they all hiked on up. It was quite a surprise party for Scott – he couldn't believe his mom would do that. Later he walked her back down and managed to get the jeep at the right angle for the drive back down.

It was a wonderful summer, watching the birds and the animals as well as the forest around us. We put out a salt lick for the deer and loved to see them come and go, and we had hundreds of chipmunks. With our binoculars, we could see elk grazing below us in the Swampy Lakes area. Also, that summer, the Olympic ski team had come to Bend to practice at Mt. Bachelor, and we could see them as little dots when they skied down. It was a quiet and carefree time. We read books, did some writing, and I even decided to try my hand at painting. I had fallen in love with the South Sister and wanted to capture my version of it. To this day, when I look at that mountain I can remember trying to paint the glaciers a certain purplish color. Originally, I had planned to work in town at Sambo's for a few days a week and then hike back up the mountain for the remainder of the time. But, after a short while I couldn't bear to leave my idyllic spot, overlooking that beautiful forest to come in and listen to customers complain about their orders of pancakes and two eggs over easy. I was having too much fun cooking our own breakfasts on the wood stove and living the pioneer girl life, so I quit the job in town.

There were no cell phones in 1964, no iPods, GPS systems or miniature TVs. Our only connection with the outside world was the walkie talkie, and we were supposed to use that only for business. Our calling code was Sugar

102, and several times a day Scott called dispatch to report activity or lack of it. One evening after we had signed off for the night, an informal call came through that there was going to be a party at Elk Lake. Everyone was invited, so we literally bounded down the mountain in record time. It was fun to meet up with the people we only knew by phone, plus we got to drink beer with them and we weren't even the legal age for it. The next morning we had to climb back up before sunrise, and we weren't quite so bouncy, but we made it in time for the check in call at 7:00 AM.

The summer season does not last long at high elevations, and we had a big snowstorm late in August. Even though it cleared the next day, we received the call to close up the lookout and they would send someone to bring us down. We really only had two months up there, but the experience gave me lasting memories. The very next year, Tumalo Mountain was one of the lookouts that was shut down permanently, and they began using planes to spot for fires after lightning storms hit. The Forest Service closed the chapter on Tumalo Mountain and many other small lookout towers. The building was burned, and hiking to the top of the mountain now, you would not even know that a structure had been there unless you knew where to look. I hike up every few years just to look around and remember. Some melted glass and a few big nails are about the only items I have found. And now they are rebuilding one of the old lookouts as part of a Forest Service exhibit at the High Desert Museum. It's funny to think that in my life, I was a part of something that is now considered historical.

Sue in front of the Tumalo Mountain Lookout

ACKNOWLEDGEMENTS

Special thanks to Rebecca Jaynes for her editing and insightful comments.

Also, I want to thank my friends in the Writing Sojourners group who were so supportive in encouraging me to publish this memoir.

ABOUT THE AUTHOR

Sue Fountain was born in Bend, Oregon in 1945 in the old St. Charles Hospital on Franklin Avenue. She attended grade school at Reid/Thompson and Kenwood before entering Bend Junior High School which was located on Wall Street where the District Administration Building is now housed. In 1961 she entered Bend Senior High School, the only high school in town, and graduated from there in 1963. As an adult, Sue divided her time between raising four children and attending college. She received her B.A. and teaching certificate from The Evergreen State College, and her Masters from Western Washington University. After teaching high school for fifteen years in Port Townsend, Washington, she felt the high desert sun calling her back to Bend. This has been her home since 2006, and not a day goes by that she is not happy to be where she is.